Thoughts on Tonight

poems by

Nathan J. Reid

Finishing Line Press
Georgetown, Kentucky

Thoughts on Tonight

Copyright © 2017 by Nathan J. Reid
ISBN 978-1-63534-342-7 First Edition
All rights reserved under International and Pan-American Copyright Conventions.
No part of this book may be reproduced in any manner whatsoever without written permission from the publisher, except in the case of brief quotations embodied in critical articles and reviews.

ACKNOWLEDGMENTS

The author would like to thank the editors of the following journal where these poems first appeared:

Fox Cry Review, Menasha, Wisconsin; "Tired and Listening to Tom Waits" and "I-94 Alone"

Publisher: Leah Maines

Editor: Christen Kincaid

Cover Art and Design: Alaina Katarina Albaugh

Author Photo: Ashley E. Beranek

Printed in the USA on acid-free paper.
Order online: www.finishinglinepress.com
also available on amazon.com

Author inquiries and mail orders:
Finishing Line Press
P. O. Box 1626
Georgetown, Kentucky 40324
U. S. A.

Table of Contents

- Heart & Feather 1
- Music Lovers 2
- Song with No Name 3
- Tired and Listening to Tom Waits 4
- Best Compliment, Or: What Katy Said to Me While
  Driving Her Home in June 5
- I-94 Alone 6
- In the Bonfire 7
- Thoughts on Tonight 8
- Oshkosh Overnight 9
- Bonfire Brown 10
- First Meditation 12
- I Be 13
- Pillow Light 14
- Pillow Locked 15
- Smelling Rain 16
- Finding Syntax 17
- Meteor 18
- Supernova's Aftermath 19
- Into Existence 20
- Waking Sleep 21
- Postmortem 22
- He Climbs Out the Cave 24
- When You Wake 26
- 7 P.M. 27
- Heavy & Exhausted 28

*To E,
without whom.*

Heart & Feather

I hide my heart in a purple silk cavern.
When underground rivers flood
I take it out, drop it in a boat,
let the water push us down a leather mountainside.
My hand trails behind me as feathers fall
through the moonlight of a birdless sky.
The wind sticks to my face like tapioca pudding. Tastes like it too.
When I feel young once again I carry my heart and boat back up the mountain,
wait inside until the next season of floods.

~   ~   ~

I have long since stopped returning to the cave,
forgot the mountain by folding up its map
until it disappeared between my fingers,
swallowed my heart back into my chest
and now sleep beneath this soup called Heavens
where showers of shooting stars rain behind my eyelids,
where tiny birds emerge from my mouth, sing into the ears of my still-yesterday self
then flap their new ingredients toward the sky.

Come morning, my first breath will be a feather in which to contemplate,
brushing its soft vanes through tomorrow.

Music Lovers

a single moment
        frozen in its own epiphany
new and unheard

we can't help but
        silence our selfish consciousness
        give our full attention
forget how our own hearts beat

ears long rusted shut
        now open
address everything else as hush

this moment evokes reverence we can only attempt
        in concert halls

eternal fragments inhale our breath
        exist through us
        exist exactly for that purpose
then let us go before we're ready

before any of us realize what's been played
        and what can still be sung

Song with No Name

Sometimes the earth is a black background
slid behind random people and furniture.

Wood carvings ripple into existence,
leave splinters of whittled life.

The roof is leaking.
Bamboo houses howl like Japanese banjos.

Bird men spread ever-encircling wings.
Feathers slide into full irises, framing portals of random futures.

Now here's that Spanish waltz I can't remember the name to.
The one the naked Catalina once belly-danced into my lap.

Tired and Listening to Tom Waits

dank heart gurgles sticky valvey
the lamp light discomforting and dim

fifty sandy beggars skid a foot across the pavement
in rhythm with the shuffle and slide, one, two
I do, one, two
alone along the floorboards on East Kimball Street

one
two
step

into a trance

wiggle waggle woozy goofy shaman
melting like aurora borealis through each position
malleable as the physics, one, two
at the beginning, one, two
of the universe, one, two

and hold

snap my thighs, slap my fingers
I'm talking Spanglish up the wall
ooga booga Señorita nice to meet ya
get sexy with the bass line, one, two

now jig

Best Compliment, Or: What Katy Said to Me While Driving Her Home in June

She said,
This is going to sound kind of weird but you know what?
This wouldn't be a bad death.
Driving here on the highway, eating a frosty, listening to Tom Waits.
I'd be okay dying right now on this drive with you.

You'd be a good person to die with.

I-94 Alone

My hand falls on the passenger seat
where your hand should be
makes a gentle fist
as a mountain of piano chords
rumbles up and down your moonbeams
carries me home.

I never take my eyes off the road.

In the Bonfire

long yellow tongues curl up and down a silhouette log
strip away bark with crackling licks

the metal basin wavers in fiery fur
collects fallen ash amid an orange glow
amid tiny dunes and lemon lava pits

a dome of wicked dancing heat

Thoughts on Tonight

Our book order came in so Ashley and I drove to Nut Squad to pick it up.
When we arrived, Harper passed me a copy of *Oz* while my dad fed songs
    to the stereo.
We had the news on mute and talked about the art of the conman,
how presidential candidates can escape foreign debt by selling government
    information,
how citizens watch every history-repeating chapter unfold, notebooks
    closed.

Afterward, we gave my dad a ride home. As our car swam through the
    city grid
I told him how I liked *Abbey Road* as a kid. He told me it made sense then
I got into theatre when I grew up. He did not expound on this.

I was lost in my own thoughts of how virtual reality might end up being
    good for humanity
in that it might train us to pay better attention to our surroundings.
I thought about adults and how they have conflicting definitions for terms
    like *deus ex machina*.
I thought about Ashley, about how rare it is to be anything in this universe.
How rare to have seen her light.

Ashley and I drove back to Madison on purple diesel.
Great sunset song: Sun King.
Good funeral song too.
We talked about the art of the present moment and how wondrous the
    world felt
when the curious mind and the child at heart played make-believe with
    the night.

Oshkosh Overnight

Ink bombs surround the planet, release their contents over the course
of minestrone soup, Roman feasts on 6th Street, false vomitoriums,
stoned litigation, the bridge that sang a soul to sleep.

The dresser speaks with a stack of Beatles albums hidden in its jowls,
wish-dreams in its throat.

Sponges absorb the black silk in time to spot yesterday's socks
next to our cell phones and loose staples in the box spring.

Shirtless, we discuss the meaning of a bedsheet.

Bonfire Brown

You're on the left side of the bed. I am on the right.
A vanilla candle roasts across the room, illuminating with an olive glow
your bare shoulder peeking out from under the blanket.

Two nude spoons roll in a heavy napkin.
I curl my arm around your waist, caress the bottom of your left breast.
Your hand arrives at my face
like five golden leaves gliding onto a gentle pond.
You turn my way, rose petal lips, a kiss.

We nestle into a pillow gaze
strung together by the one light reflected in both our eyes.
As stars live and give a motley existence
so your irises breathe fiery truth, in an earthly hue.
I find myself exposed and elated in the view of bonfire brown.

Embedded with frequent leaps of fire, rippling
with the smoke of toasting timber, your eyes
wear a rare brown born of abstract and magic
that ever burns and ever calms with endless heat—like a cryptic color
from some other-dimensional rainbow, unique as soul.
No crayon will ever bear the label, no painter will ever replicate bonfire
   brown.

Assuming a sacrosanct pose, we even up our eyebrows,
pet nose with nose. A kiss. Eyes closed,
we bathe ourselves in secret prayers only two can share.
A silent washing away of wishes now come true.

Deep in meditation, my mind gasps.
I can feel that sense-of-something-higher
connecting our carnal coil
to every ancient pocket
in every curved corner of the universe.
And I find how the answer to every cosmic question is bonfire brown.

Another kiss.
Nibbling my bottom lip, smirking like a frisky kitten
you say, "What do you call a spectacular spasm?"
With a voluntary neck-twitch, I reply, "A fantas-*tic*!"
A better kiss. I continue with,
"What do you call a glorious grossness?"
Feigning a disgusted frown you return, "A fantast-*ick*!"
Giggle fits, a longer kiss.

Then your honey crisp cheeks fall just slightly,
sobering thoughts struggle with tipsy words
and with a bold healthy bit of fear you ask me,
"What is love?"

Like those miraculous moments
when two raindrops are two yet two raindrops are one
I lean in again with not just a kiss but all of me to all of you.

Vanilla's glow, middle of the bed
you have sunrise in your smile and a sunset in each brown eye.
With my naked hand cradling your naked face, I confess,
"Dearest dreamy darling: love is bonfire brown."

We mold the blanket up around us.
Two nude spoons rolling in a cozy calm.
Before the olive light is gone: good night lips, a kiss.

First Meditation

She climbs out the honey pot to come cover me with kisses.
When our skins touch the cold bedrock turns balmy beneath our toes.
Eternity chased us as we burrowed through countless synapses
like blind thoughts trying to imagine.
Now we stand in crystal splendor,
sway to the rain outside, to Ravi Shankar and Norah Jones.
Honey drips from naked as-you-wishes
while a rhythm is unearthed from neighboring stars above,
pulling us along like daring waves at sea.

We live in a spaceship made of stone.

I Be

jazzy, dreaming
counting stars instead of sheep
wishing on one of them
soft guitar strums shedding warmth
strings of handsome two-word phrases
quiet
a gentle pulse
an auburn sigh
firm, comfy
a touch of drool
heavy wonder
an open window breeze
mumbling half-consciously
teddy, honey kisses, a faithful cuddle
and did I mention asleep
with sheets, dreaming
I be

Pillow Light

Her hair sometimes smelled liked orange cough drops.

Saturday windows kept tableaus too bright.
I remember her still-life bosom, how its charged-up skin looked
in naked walks from our bed to the shower.
I would joke in my worst Monty Python impression,
crudely go back and forth about the weather
and how my William Tells gave call to her dairy cows—*Splendid!*
Then she would swoop into me until we were both dying phoenixes,
bowing to each other before bursting into flames.

Pillow Locked

Bed was a riverboat
drifting on last night's soft music,
propping us back onto our feet by morning.

But when she moved her lips again, the script was lost.
In our absent dialogue history had no choice
but to remove the I love yous from her mouth.

Smelling Rain

Tornado sirens went off five times tonight.
Thunderstorms atone in a funnel cloud's wake.

Nicki sleeps a distant sleep, eyes tucked into carefree cushions.
The open window frames me.
I watch a shallow ditch fill with the chatter of rain
as smooth wind drips train sounds over my face.
The dark apartment flickers.
Nicki doesn't stir. Safe.

Electrostatic air ignites jumbled thoughts:

sweet, cigarette, barefoot, puddles, skippy,
prospect, avenue, peanut, butter, ice, cream, pigtails,
ponytail, suicidal, soul, mate, tom, boy, girl, cat,
first love, deaf rape, big hurts, big hearts,
recoveries, boundaries, backrubs, wild hikes,
pokes, shoves, bites, shared food, like minds, short flights,
long hugs, whirlwinds, maple trees, Escher worlds, asparagus,
soft sighs, lost time,

rain.

Mineral aromas hang below the windowsill.
Silent seeds of parsley, onions, tomatoes are all sprouting.
The fleeting river in the ditch pools as fast as it drains.

Only rocks will be left by morning.

Finding Syntax

words whisper in darkness
lightly bump into each other
kissing letter to letter

...want...you...happy...

no real order
a simple message
looping over and over

...just...want...you...happy...

no real time
shadowy voices with buzzing outlines
who spoke? who is speaking?

...just...want...you...

floating breath
raw as a shaky confession
wonders just how

...happy

Meteor

drips stardust
puncturing skies with ferocious hope

whispers
meet me
at the other end
of the universe

twinkle twinkle
little dreams

explode

Supernova's Aftermath

every nebula bows to the black hole

the whirlpool reaches out
clutches all those trinkets of the universe
holds them close to its chest
compresses them into a single moment
without worry, without time

it's not evil
it merely wants to maintain melting visions
the way all observers do, hide them
preserve them with eternal revelry
cherish them for their absoluteness
like Hawking's theory of everything

Into Existence

a skull blossom
>blending light and thought

inspiration caught
>in the cranium

blooms in a blink
>like a brand-new universe

it is beyond your own flesh
>your cradled electric heart

it pumps creation
>into a complex system of love

infinity's eyes
>emit stardust
pollinate reality with winged dreams

butterflies chase bullets
>and eventually surpass them

Waking Sleep

In dreams I awake
wriggle in reality

hunting and fleeing truth

then doze once more
into the slumbers of daily routine.

Postmortem

i

He could look back.
He could stand at the beginning and look forward.
He could watch diners pass around ceramic cups of black coffee,
could watch locks of hair from one person's head find another person's shoulder.
He could see the mosaic emotions from every world he had ever met,
the tears never drying, the laughter never growing old.

ii

He enjoyed looking at it all from the side
where music blooms into stalagmite sounds that musicians once heard dripping from above,
where angry war slithers along with its severed head,
where art moves through an old theatre like a majestic whale resurfacing to breathe,
where every life is the eye of an hourglass
and those sweet permanent streaks of comet tails
burst with all the complexity the universe leaves behind while passing through a single soul.

iii

His thoughts run a straight line through curved space.
The cones in his eyes wrap infinity arcs around his mind,
sweeping nows and thens like a hyperspatial pendulum.
He once heard the chatter of innocent starlight,
it blipped out blueprints for time machines which he wrote down and posted on the fridge.
Four time machine settings become obvious to old souls and young minds:
Past, Present, Future, and Meanwhile.

iv

The concrete world began to spin, condensate,
flow in and out of itself in thick clouds of remembrance.
He went not to his last moments but to his favorite moments:
He is laughing at a funeral.
He is reading his first science fiction.
He is a midnight vow on his honeymoon too sacred for the ears of
 witnesses.
He is brotherly love sharing a booth with joyous friends, passing good
 stories over damn good food.
He is in rehearsal, directing.
He is a genius child with eyes of roaring sapphire,
new thoughts appear to him like strange ghosts escaping the space-
 time vortex,
they whisper random details of a happy life.
He is smiling.

v

The only noise is streetlight.
He considers all these things: the laughter audible, the nows even
 closer than before.
He is in a warm bed, his book bookmarked.
A shooting star flickers briefly in the inked sky.
The shell falls to Earth.
The light shines.
Onward.

He Climbs Out the Cave

on his belly
bleeding
his cut-covered body swimming through gravel and warm light

blood flows freely
its red trail swallowed down a black throat
to the rumbling guts of catacombs
back to the beginning
where dark pools dream

he crawls to a rest under the hot sun
whispers to the dirt
makes a bed of his thoughts
wheezes
then sleeps

the wind lifts a small weight from his wounds

he awakes to starlight
exhausted

though he's never seen the sky before
he recognizes a solitary white orb
twinkling *déjà vu*
it unlocks visions in his deep and ancient memory:
that same white glow
remained beside him many years
then rose
from warm hands
rose from breath and a heartbeat
out of reach of the pools and dreams
rose farther
lighter than air
until finally
vanishing

he realizes the dust of night
how it takes time to float
to catch wonder in its motley shine

he looks back into the open mouth of absence and nothingness
knowing he shall not return

the landscape changes to a familiar voice

his mind sinks inside a tattered shell
silver circuitry retreating its branches into a ball of pure energy

it glows
weightless
responding to that ancient voice
then finally
rises

When You Wake

you hear distant rumors about what it will be like
to go to sleep and never wake up

about a time when all vibrations cash in their casino chips, take the red-
 eye home
when the biggest number is again smaller than the smallest number
when your mind is a wilting flower
and an hour yet pending returns you to the realm that fed you into birth

you hear these things happening someday

but today you breathe fire and music as if fire and music, like yourself,
were somehow separate from this collapsing dream of time trying to
 remember light

you have always been light
light is the reality beneath the dream

as you are breath you are the nothingness
a photon knows not its own existence

so why fear the wilted flower?

if the color has gone pallid
the leaves too brittle to touch
then cheer the fragrance

it is still so incredible and lovely

7 P.M.

We are lounging on the sofa.
I am wearing my Tardis pants.
She is tracing not just the outline of a blue box but all its details.
She does this for several minutes.
The whole time I pretend she is secretly writing me a love letter
and even though it is her finger carving out each word from my leg
by the end I'm the only one who knows what her message says.

Heavy & Exhausted

Tonight I could sleep
as if an anvil were a prayer I was making

as if my own body heat
were a kiss of jasmine

as if peace were a feather
composed of you, them, me

to be found balanced on my nose
when I wake.

Spoken word poet **Nathan J. Reid** was born in a house on Amherst Avenue, in the "on the water" city of Oshkosh, Wisconsin, where he grew up with a big family and a penchant for writing and theatre. He joined the Eclectic Arts Ensemble Theatre Company as a teenager and spent several years acting, directing, playwriting, set-building, and engaging in many other aspects of the art form. His first published poem appeared in *Teen Ink Magazine*, and his work has been subsequently published in the *Penguin Review, Fox Cry Review, Binnacle*, as well as other journals. He is also a former senior editor for the *Wisconsin Review*.

Reid's poetry is born out of a simple yet strong passion to strive for and share inner truth. Constantly rooting for the good in people, he explores aspects of human nature both sweet and bittersweet to create art that has an ultimately hopeful message. He believes the truth of one individual can ignite new truth in another, and that this process of sharing and discovering truth forwards the human condition in a direction that is positive, honest, and intelligent.

He currently lives in Madison, Wisconsin with his partner, Ashley, and their ever-growing library of books. He is a regularly featured spoken word artist for various events around the state and competes in poetry slams whenever he can. In addition to artistic pursuits, Nathan is an avid reader, occasional songwriter, amateur philosopher, and enthusiast of movies, quiz shows, travel, and chocolate.

Visit him at nathanjreid.com for more information.

www.ingramcontent.com/pod-product-compliance
Lightning Source LLC
LaVergne TN
LVHW041514070426
835507LV00012B/1560